Delicious Pork Recipes for Every Occasion

From Slow-Cooked Ribs to Quick and Easy Pork Chops,
Discover the Ultimate Pork Cookbook for Meat Lovers!

BY Terra Compasso

Licensing and Copyrighting

Table of Contents

Introduction

Delicious pork Recipes for Every Occasion is a complete guide to cooking with one of the most versatile meats available - pig! Many people enjoy pork because of its excellent flavor, juicy texture, and variety of methods to prepare it. We have prepared a variety of exquisite pork dishes in this book that will fulfill your appetites while also allowing you to explore new culinary boundaries.

This book covers a wide range of hog recipes, from familiar staples like pork chops and bacon to cosmopolitan delicacies like Mexican carnitas and Chinese char siu. Whether you're cooking for yourself, your family, or a dinner party, this book has you covered with simple recipes and helpful hints.

1. Cold Saimin Salad with Soy-Ginger Grilled Pork

This Cold Saimin Salad with Soy-Ginger Grilled Pork is a refreshing and satisfying dish perfect for warm weather. The thin noodles are mixed with fresh vegetables and tossed in a tangy dressing, while the soy-ginger grilled pork adds a flavorful and protein-packed punch.

Preparation Time: 1 hour

Serves: 6

Ingredients:

- 1/4 cup of vegetable oil (60 milliliters)
- 1/4 teaspoon of black pepper (1 gram)
- 1/4 cup of chopped peanuts (30 grams)
- 1/2 teaspoon of salt (2.5 grams)
- 2 garlic cloves, minced
- 1/2 cup of sliced carrots (50 grams)
- 1/4 cup of soy sauce (60 milliliters)
- 1/2 cup of sliced red bell pepper (50 grams)
- 1/4 cup of honey (85 grams)
- 1/2 cup of sliced green onions (50 grams)
- 1/4 cup of rice vinegar (60 milliliters)
- 2 tablespoons of grated ginger (30 grams)
- 1/2 cup of sliced cucumbers (50 grams)
- 1/4 cup of chopped cilantro (10 grams)
- 1 pound of saimin noodles (453 grams)
- 1 pound of pork tenderloin (453 grams)

xxxxxxxxxxxxxxxxxxxxxxxxxxxxxxxxxxxxxxxxxxxxxxx

Instructions:

    a. Set the grill's temperature to medium-high.

    b. Soy sauce, honey, minced garlic, ginger, rice vinegar, vegetable oil, salt, and black pepper should all be combined in a mixing bowl. For later use, set aside 1/4 cup of the marinade.

    c. Toss the pork tenderloin with the marinade in a mixing dish to coat. For 30 minutes, marinate.

    d. Turn the pork tenderloin on the grill for 15 to 20 minutes, or until it reaches an internal temperature of 145°F (63°C). Prior to slicing, let the pork to rest for 5 minutes.

    e. Saimin noodles should be prepared in the interim per the directions on the box. Rinse with cold water after draining.

    f. The cooked saimin noodles, chopped cilantro, chopped peanuts, green onions, carrots, and cucumbers should all be combined in a large mixing dish.

    g. Add the reserved 1/4 cup of marinade to the mixing bowl and toss to combine.

    h. Serve the saimin salad with the sliced soy-ginger grilled pork on top.

    i. Enjoy!

2. Mustard and Lemon-Glazed Pork with Roasted Vegetables

Mustard and lemon-glazed pork is a delicious dish that combines tangy flavors with succulent pork. The glaze is made with Dijon mustard, lemon juice, and honey, which creates a sweet and savory taste. Served with roasted vegetables, this meal is both healthy and satisfying.

Preparation Time: 1 hour 30 minutes

Serves: 8

Ingredients:

- 1 tsp salt
- 1 tsp salt
- 1 tbsp dried thyme
- 2 kg pork loin
- 1/2 cup honey
- 1 tsp black pepper
- 1 tsp black pepper
- 1 tbsp fresh thyme leaves
- 1/4 cup olive oil
- 1 kg mixed vegetables (carrots, potatoes, onions, bell peppers)
- 1/2 cup Dijon mustard
- 1/4 cup lemon juice
- 2 tbsp olive oil
- 1 tbsp garlic powder

xxxxxxxxxxxxxxxxxxxxxxxxxxxxxxxxxxxxxxxxxxxxxxx

Instructions:

a. Set the oven's temperature to 180 /350.

b. Mix the Dijon mustard, honey, lemon juice, olive oil, dried thyme, garlic powder, salt, and pepper in a mixing bowl.

c. Put the pork loin in a roasting pan and cover the meat with the mustard and lemon glaze.

d. Using a meat thermometer, roast the pork for 1 hour, or until it reaches an internal temperature of 63°C/145°F.

e. While the meat roasts, prepare the vegetables. After chopping the vegetables into bite-sized pieces, place them on a baking sheet. Season with salt, black pepper, and olive oil to taste. Toss to coat.

f. After the pork has been roasting for 30 minutes, add the vegetables to the oven and roast for another 30 minutes, or until tender and caramelized.

g. The pork and vegetables should be removed from the oven and rested for 10 minutes before slicing.

h. Serve the sliced pork with roasted vegetables and fresh thyme leaves on top.

3. Barbecued Pulled Pork

Barbecued pulled pork is a classic dish that is loved for its smoky flavor and tender texture. Slow-cooked and coated in a tangy barbecue sauce, the pork becomes infused with a rich flavor that makes it perfect for sandwiches or as a standalone dish. It's the ultimate comfort food.

Preparation Time: 20 minutes

Serves: 10

Ingredients:

- 1 tbsp (5 ml) a pinch of garlic powder
- 1 tsp (5 ml) garlic powder
- 1/4 cup (60 ml) dark brown sugar
- 1/2 cup (120 ml) vinegar made from apple cider
- 1/2 tsp (2.5 ml) 1/4 teaspoon of salt
- 3 lbs. (1.4 kg) roast boneless pork shoulder
- 1/2 tsp (2.5 ml) paprika with a smokey flavor
- 1/2 tsp (1.25 ml) black pepper
- 1 cup (240 ml) sauce for barbecuing
- 1/2 cup (120 ml) chicken stock
- 1 tbsp (15 ml) 1 teaspoon Dijon mustard
- 1 tbsp (15 ml) Sauce with Worcestershire sauce

xxxxxxxxxxxxxxxxxxxxxxxxxxxxxxxxxxxxxxxxxxxxxxx

Instructions:

a. BBQ sauce, apple cider vinegar, chicken broth, brown sugar, Worcestershire sauce, Dijon mustard, garlic powder, onion powder, smoked paprika, salt, and black pepper should all be combined in a mixing bowl.

b. Put the slow cooker's pork shoulder roast inside.

c. Over the pork shoulder roast, pour the barbecue sauce mixture.

d. Cook the food in the slow cooker with the lid on for 8–10 hours on low or 4–6 hours on high.

e. Shred the pork shoulder roast with a fork after removing it from the slow cooker.

f. After mixing the barbecue sauce, add the shredded pork back to the slow cooker.

g. Cook on low heat for a further 30 minutes.

h. Serve hot on buns or rolls.

4. Pork Loin Roast with Caramelized Onions and White Wine–Dijon Sauce

Pork loin roast with caramelized onions and white wine-Dijon sauce is a mouthwatering dish that combines juicy pork with sweet onions and a flavorful sauce. The pork is cooked to perfection and the caramelized onions add a touch of sweetness that pairs perfectly with the tangy sauce. It's a crowd-pleasing meal that's perfect for a special occasion.

Preparation Time: 2 hours

Serves: 8

Ingredients:

- 1/2 teaspoon black pepper
- 1/2 cup white wine
- 2 tablespoons Dijon mustard
- 1 (4-5 pound) boneless pork loin roast
- 2 tablespoons chopped fresh parsley
- 1 teaspoon salt
- 1/2 cup chicken broth
- 2 large onions, thinly sliced
- 2 tablespoons butter
- 1 tablespoon olive oil

xxxxxxxxxxxxxxxxxxxxxxxxxxxxxxxxxxxxxxxxxxxxxxxxx

Instructions:

a. Oven temperature should be set at 375°F (190°C).

b. Over medium-high heat, warm up the olive oil in a large skillet. Salt and black pepper should be used to season the roast pork loin. About 5 minutes should be spent on each side to brown the pork loin roast in the pan.

c. Place the pork loin roast in a roasting pan, then wrap it in foil. For one hour, roast in the oven.

d. In the meantime, melt butter in the same pan over medium heat. After adding, sauté the onions in the pan for about 20 minutes, or until they are caramelized.

e. Pour white wine into the skillet and swirl to deglaze it. Add chicken broth and Dijon mustard after stirring. Bring to a boil and cook for 10 minutes or until just slightly thickened.

f. Roast pork loin should be taken out of the oven and exposed. Apply the white wine-Dijon sauce on the top. Return the roast to the oven and roast uncovered for a further 30 minutes, or until a meat thermometer reads 145°F (63°C) inside.

g. Prior to slicing, give the pork loin roast a 10-minute rest. Serve with any residual white wine-Dijon sauce and fresh parsley that has been chopped.

5. Busiate with Pork Ragù

Busiate with pork ragù is a traditional Italian pasta dish that is full of rich flavors. The pasta is served with a delicious ragù made from slow-cooked pork, tomatoes, and a blend of herbs and spices. The result is a hearty and comforting meal that is perfect for any occasion.

Preparation Time: 2 hours

Serves: 8

Ingredients:

- 1-pound (450g) Busiate pasta
- 1/4 cup (60ml) grated Parmesan cheese
- 1/2 teaspoon (2g) black pepper
- 1 pound (450g) ground pork
- 1 teaspoon (5g) salt
- 1/4 teaspoon (1g) red pepper flakes
- 1 onion, chopped
- 3 cloves garlic, minced
- 1 can (28oz/800g) crushed tomatoes
- 1/2 cup (120ml) red wine
- 2 tablespoons (30ml) olive oil
- 1/4 cup (60ml) chopped fresh parsley

xxxxxxxxxxxxxxxxxxxxxxxxxxxxxxxxxxxxxxxxxxxxxx

Instructions:

a. Cook the Busiate spaghetti as directed on the box, then drain and leave aside.
b. Warm the olive oil in a large pan over medium heat. Cook, stirring periodically, until the ground pork is browned.
c. Cook until the onion is translucent, approximately 5 minutes, in the skillet with the chopped onion and minced garlic.
d. Pour in the red wine and smashed tomatoes, then season with salt, black pepper, and red pepper flakes. To blend, stir everything together thoroughly.
e. Reduce the heat to low and simmer the sauce for 1 hour, stirring periodically.
f. Stir in the chopped parsley after the sauce has thickened.
g. Serve the Busiate pasta with the pork ragù and Parmesan cheese on top.

6. Pork Chops with Sunflower Seed Gremolata

Pork chops with sunflower seed gremolata is a unique and flavorful dish that combines the richness of pork with the nuttiness of sunflower seeds. The gremolata, made with sunflower seeds, lemon zest, garlic, and parsley, adds a bright and fresh flavor to the pork. It's a delicious and easy-to-make meal.

Preparation Time: 45 minutes

Serves: 4

Ingredients:

- half a cup sunflower seed
- 4 pork chops, bone-in (about 1 inch thick)
- 1/2 cup chopped fresh parsley
- 1/4 teaspoon ground black pepper
- 2 tbsp of olive oil
- 2 minced garlic cloves
- 1/4 cup chopped fresh mint
- 1 teaspoon of salt

xxxxxxxxxxxxxxxxxxxxxxxxxxxxxxxxxxxxxxxxxxxxxxx

Instructions:

a. Oven temperature should be set at 375°F (190°C).

b. Sunflower seeds should be spread out on a baking sheet and baked for 5 to 7 minutes, or until fragrant and gently browned. Remove from the oven, then allow to cool.

c. The toasted sunflower seeds, parsley, mint, garlic, salt, and pepper should all be thoroughly minced in a food processor before being combined. Put aside in a small basin after transfer.

d. Salt and pepper should be used to season the pork chops.

e. Over medium-high heat, warm up the olive oil in a large skillet. Add the pork chops and cook for 4–5 minutes on each side, or until browned and done.

f. Serve the pork chops with gremolata made from sunflower seeds on top.

7. Pork Chop au Poivre with Red Wine– Shallot Sauce

Pork chop au poivre with red wine-shallot sauce is a classic French dish that is full of flavor. The pork chops are coated with peppercorns and pan-seared to perfection, then served with a rich red wine and shallot sauce. The result is a decadent and satisfying meal that's perfect for a special occasion.

Preparation Time: 45 minutes

Serves: 2

Ingredients:

- 1/2 teaspoon salt
- 1 tablespoon unsalted butter
- 1/2 cup red wine
- 1 shallot, finely chopped
- 2 bone-in pork chops (3/4 inch thick)
- 1 tablespoon olive oil
- 1/2 cup beef broth
- 1 tablespoon black peppercorns

xxxxxxxxxxxxxxxxxxxxxxxxxxxxxxxxxxxxxxxxxxxxxx

Instructions:

a. Using a heavy skillet or a meat mallet, crush the peppercorns. Salt and peppercorns should be used to season pork chops.

b. Over medium-high heat, warm up the olive oil in a big skillet. Pork chops should be added and cooked for 4 minutes on each side, or until browned and done. Transfer to a platter, then maintain warmth.

c. Shallot should be added to the same pan and cooked for 2 minutes or until tender. Bring to a boil the beef broth and red wine additions. Reduce heat, cover, and simmer for five minutes or until sauce slightly thickens.

d. Butter should be added to the skillet and stirred until melted. Serve red wine-shallot sauce with the pork chops.

8. Thit Kho – Vietnamese Braised Pork Belly

Thit kho is a traditional Vietnamese dish that features succulent pork belly braised in a flavorful sauce made with caramelized sugar, fish sauce, and spices. The dish is typically served with rice and pickled vegetables, and the result is a rich and savory meal that's perfect for any occasion.

Preparation Time: 30 minutes

Serves: 4

Ingredients:

- 1 tablespoon fish sauce
- 1/2 cup water
- 500g pork belly, sliced into 1-inch pieces
- 3 cloves garlic, minced
- 1 tablespoon soy sauce
- 1 tablespoon sugar
- 1/2 teaspoon salt
- 2 tablespoons vegetable oil
- 1/2 teaspoon black pepper
- 1 shallot, sliced

xxxxxxxxxxxxxxxxxxxxxxxxxxxxxxxxxxxxxxxxxxxxxx

Instructions:

a. In a large pot, heat the vegetable oil over medium-high heat.
b. Add the garlic and shallot and sauté for 1-2 minutes until fragrant.
c. Add the sliced pork belly and cook until browned on all sides.
d. Add the sugar, fish sauce, soy sauce, black pepper, salt, and water to the pot.
e. Stir to combine and bring to a boil.
f. Reduce the heat to low and cover the pot with a lid.
g. Simmer for 30-40 minutes, stirring occasionally, until the pork belly is tender, and the sauce has thickened.
h. Serve hot with steamed rice.

9. Pork Tenderloin with Charred Tomatillo Salsa

Pork tenderloin with charred tomatillo salsa is a delicious and healthy meal that is full of bold flavors. The tender pork is seasoned with a blend of spices and grilled to perfection, then served with a tangy and slightly spicy tomatillo salsa. It's a refreshing twist on a classic pork dish.

Preparation Time: 1 hour

Serves: 8

Ingredients:

- 2 pounds tomatillos, husks removed and rinsed
- 1 tablespoon garlic powder
- 1 tablespoon olive oil
- 2 jalapenos, stemmed and seeded
- 4 cloves garlic, peeled
- Juice of 1 lime
- 1/4 cup chopped cilantro
- 1/2 teaspoon black pepper
- 2 pork tenderloins (about 2 pounds)
- 1 tablespoon smoked paprika
- 1 teaspoon salt
- 1 large onion, sliced into thick rounds
- Salt and pepper, to taste
- 1 tablespoon chili powder

xxxxxxxxxxxxxxxxxxxxxxxxxxxxxxxxxxxxxxxxxxxxx

Instructions:

a. Heat the grill to a medium-high setting.

b. Combine chili powder, smoked paprika, garlic powder, olive oil, salt, and black pepper in a small bowl.

c. The pork tenderloins should be well covered in the spice mixture.

d. Grill the pork tenderloins for 20 to 25 minutes, or until a meat thermometer reads 145°F (63°C).

e. The pork tenderloins should be taken from the grill and given 5 minutes to rest before being cut into rounds that are 1/2 inch thick.

f. Prepare the salsa while the pork is roasting. On the grill, add the tomatillos, onion, jalapenos, and garlic. Cook for 10 to 15 minutes, turning occasionally, until browned all over.

g. Place the charred veggies in a food processor and process until smooth.

h. Add cilantro, lime juice, and salt & pepper to taste.

i. Serve the sliced pork tenderloin with the charred tomatillo salsa.

10. Pork Loin Stuffed with Pesto and Prosciutto

Pork loin stuffed with pesto and prosciutto is an elegant dish that is sure to impress. The pork is butterflied and filled with a mixture of fresh pesto and thinly sliced prosciutto, then roasted to perfection. The result is a flavorful and juicy pork dish that's perfect for a special occasion.

Preparation Time: 1 hour 30 minutes

Serves: 8

Ingredients:

- 8 thin slices prosciutto
- 1/4 cup grated Parmesan cheese
- 1 tablespoon olive oil
- 1/4 cup chopped fresh parsley
- 1 (3-pound) boneless pork loin
- 1/2 cup pesto
- Freshly ground black pepper and salt

xxxxxxxxxxxxxxxxxxxxxxxxxxxxxxxxxxxxxxxxxxxxxx

Instructions:

a. Preheat oven to 375°F (190°C).

b. Butterfly the pork loin by cutting it lengthwise down the center, stopping 1/2 inch from the bottom.

c. Open the pork loin like a book and pound it to an even thickness.

d. Spread the pesto over the pork loin.

e. Layer the prosciutto over the pesto.

f. Sprinkle the Parmesan cheese and parsley over the prosciutto.

g. Roll the pork loin tightly and tie it with kitchen twine at 1-inch intervals.

h. Rub the olive oil over the pork loin and season with pepper and salt.

i. Place the pork loin in a roasting pan and roast for 1 hour or until a meat thermometer inserted into the thickest part registers 145°F (63°C).

j. Remove the pork loin from the oven and let it rest for 10 minutes before slicing and serving.

11. Crispy Pork Cutlets with Tonnato Sauce

Crispy pork cutlets with tonnato sauce is a tasty and easy-to-make meal that is perfect for any night of the week. The pork cutlets are breaded and fried until crispy, then served with a tangy and creamy tonnato sauce made with anchovies, capers, and mayonnaise. It's a delicious twist on a classic pork dish.

Preparation Time: 45 minutes

Serves: 4

Ingredients:

- 1/4 teaspoon paprika
- 1/4 teaspoon garlic powder
- 1 tablespoon Dijon mustard
- 1/2 cup mayonnaise
- 1/4 cup olive oil
- 2 large eggs
- 1/2 cup grated Parmesan cheese
- 2 tablespoons lemon juice
- 1/2 cup all-purpose flour
- 2 tablespoons capers, drained and rinsed
- 4 boneless pork cutlets (about 1/2 inch thick)
- 1/2 teaspoon salt
- 1/4 teaspoon onion powder
- 1 cup panko breadcrumbs
- 1/4 teaspoon black pepper

xxxxxxxxxxxxxxxxxxxxxxxxxxxxxxxxxxxxxxxxxxxxx

Instructions:

a. Preheat oven to 375°F (190°C).

b. Use a meat mallet to pound pork cutlets to an even 1/4-inch thickness.

c. In shallow bowl, place flour. In another shallow bowl, beat eggs. In third shallow bowl, combine panko breadcrumbs, Parmesan cheese, salt, and black pepper.

d. Dredge each pork cutlet in flour, shaking off excess. Dip in egg, then coat with breadcrumb mixture, pressing lightly to adhere. Place on a baking sheet lined with parchment paper.

e. Bake pork cutlets for 15-20 minutes, until cooked through and crispy.

f. While pork is baking, prepare the tonnato sauce. In a blender or food processor, combine mayonnaise, capers, lemon juice, Dijon mustard, garlic powder, onion powder, and paprika. Blend until smooth.

g. Heat olive oil in large skillet over medium heat. Add pork cutlets and cook for 2-3 minutes per side, until golden brown and crispy.

h. Serve pork cutlets with tonnato sauce on the side.

12. Porco à Alentejana (Portuguese Braised Pork and Clams)

Porco à Alentejana is a traditional Portuguese dish that combines succulent pork with fresh clams, potatoes, and a flavorful tomato-based broth. The dish is cooked slowly to allow the flavors to meld together, resulting in a rich and savory meal that's perfect for a special occasion or a cozy night in.

Preparation Time: 2 hours

Serves: 8

Ingredients:

- 2 tbsp (30 ml) olive oil
- 1 tsp (5 ml) dried oregano
- 1 cup (240 ml) chicken broth
- 1 tsp (5 ml) paprika
- 1/2 tsp (2.5 ml) salt
- 1 tsp (5 ml) ground cumin
- 2 lbs. (900 g) pork shoulder, cut into 1-inch cubes
- 4 garlic cloves, minced
- 1 onion, chopped
- 2 bay leaves
- 1 lb. (450 g) clams, scrubbed and rinsed
- 1/4 tsp (1.25 ml) black pepper
- 1 cup (240 ml) dry white wine
- 2 tbsp (30 ml) chopped fresh parsley

xxxxxxxxxxxxxxxxxxxxxxxxxxxxxxxxxxxxxxxxxxxxxx

Instructions:

    a. Set the oven's temperature to (175°C).350°F.

    b. Olive oil should be heated over medium-high heat in a large Dutch oven or heavy-bottomed saucepan.

    c. For about 5 minutes, add the pork cubes and brown them on both sides.

    d. Take the pork out of the saucepan, then set it aside.

    e. Cook the onion and garlic in the saucepan for 3 minutes or until tender.

    f. Cook for a further minute before adding the paprika, cumin, oregano, salt, and black pepper.

    g. Bring to a boil after adding the white wine and chicken broth.

    h. Stir in the bay leaves after adding the meat back to the saucepan.

    i. Place the saucepan in the oven while it is covered.

    j. One hour of baking.

    k. Stir in the clams after adding them to the saucepan.

    l. Cover the pot and return to the oven.

    m. Bake for another 30 minutes or until the clams have opened.

    n. Discard any clams that do not open.

    o. Sprinkle with chopped parsley and serve hot.

13. Herb-Basted Pork Chops

Herb-basted pork chops are a simple yet flavorful dish that's perfect for any night of the week. The pork chops are seasoned with a blend of fresh herbs and then basted with butter to keep them juicy and tender. It's an easy-to-make meal that's sure to please everyone at the table.

Preparation Time: 30 minutes

Serves: 4

Ingredients:

- 4 bone-in pork chops (1 inch thick)
- 2 tablespoons chopped fresh rosemary
- 2 tablespoons olive oil
- Salt and black pepper to taste
- 2 garlic cloves, minced
- 2 tablespoons chopped fresh thyme
- 1/4 cup chicken broth

xxxxxxxxxxxxxxxxxxxxxxxxxxxxxxxxxxxxxxxxxxxxxxxx

Instructions:

a. Preheat oven to 400°F (200°C).

b. In a mixing bowl, combine olive oil, rosemary, thyme, garlic, salt, and black pepper.

c. Place pork chops on a baking sheet and brush herb mixture over each chop.

d. Bake for 20-25 minutes or until internal temperature reaches 145°F (63°C).

e. Remove from oven and let rest for 5 minutes.

f. In a small saucepan, heat chicken broth over medium heat.

g. Baste pork chops with chicken broth and serve.

14. Yunnan-Style Spicy Pork–Stuffed Eggplant

Yunnan-style spicy pork-stuffed eggplant is a flavorful and hearty dish that's popular in Chinese cuisine. The eggplant is stuffed with a spicy pork filling made with Sichuan peppercorns, ginger, and garlic, then simmered in a flavorful sauce. It's a comforting and satisfying meal that's perfect for cold weather.

Preparation Time: 45 minutes

Serves: 4

Ingredients:

- 2 tablespoons doubanjiang (spicy bean paste)
- 1 tablespoon vegetable oil
- 2 large eggplants
- 1 tablespoon garlic, minced
- 1/4 teaspoon ground Sichuan pepper
- 1 teaspoon sugar
- 1/4 cup chopped scallions
- 1 tablespoon soy sauce
- 1 pound ground pork
- 1/4 cup chopped cilantro
- 1 tablespoon Shaoxing wine
- 1 tablespoon ginger, minced
- 1/4 teaspoon five-spice powder

xxxxxxxxxxxxxxxxxxxxxxxxxxxxxxxxxxxxxxxxxxxx

Instructions:

a. Cut the eggplants in half lengthwise and scoop out the flesh, leaving a 1/4-inch-thick shell. Chop the flesh into small pieces and set aside.

b. Heat the vegetable oil in a wok over high heat. Add the ginger and garlic and stir-fry for 30 seconds. Add the ground pork and stir-fry until browned and cooked through, about 5 minutes.

c. Add the doubanjiang, soy sauce, Shaoxing wine, sugar, five-spice powder, and Sichuan pepper. Stir-fry for 2-3 minutes until fragrant.

d. Add the chopped eggplant, scallions, and cilantro. Stir-fry for another 2-3 minutes until the eggplant is cooked through.

e. Divide the pork mixture evenly among the eggplant halves.

f. Preheat the oven to 375°F (190°C). Place the stuffed eggplant halves on a baking sheet and bake for 15-20 minutes until the eggplant is tender and the filling is hot and bubbly.

15. Schweinebraten (German Roast Pork Shoulder)

Schweinebraten is a traditional German dish made from a pork shoulder that is marinated and roasted to perfection. The meat is seasoned with spices and served with sides such as sauerkraut and potato dumplings. It is a hearty and flavorful meal that is popular throughout Germany.

Preparation Time: 20 minutes

Serves: 8

Ingredients:

- 1 cup beef broth
- 1 tbsp black pepper
- 2 tbsp vegetable oil
- 2 tbsp paprika
- 1 tbsp caraway seeds
- 2 tbsp salt
- 4 garlic cloves, minced
- 1 (4-5 lb.) bone-in pork shoulder
- 1 onion, chopped

xxxxxxxxxxxxxxxxxxxxxxxxxxxxxxxxxxxxxxxxxxxxxxx

Instructions:

a. Set the oven to 325°F (160°C).
b. Combine the paprika, salt, caraway seeds, and black pepper in a small bowl.
c. Rub the pork shoulder all over with the spice mixture.
d. Heat the vegetable oil to a medium-high temperature in a roasting pan.
e. Brown the pork shoulder by searing it on all sides.
f. To the roasting pan, add the minced garlic and diced onion.
g. Over the pork shoulder, pour the beef broth.
h. The roasting pan should be covered with foil.
i. The pork shoulder should be roasted for 3–4 hours, or until it achieves an internal temperature of 145°F (63°C).
j. To brown the top, roast for a further 30 minutes after removing the foil.
k. Before slicing and serving, let the pork shoulder rest for ten to fifteen minutes.

16. Babi Panggang Karo (North Sumatran Grilled Pork)

Babi Panggang Karo is a popular dish from the Karo region of North Sumatra, Indonesia. It features grilled pork that has been marinated with a blend of herbs and spices, giving it a rich and savory flavor. It is often served with steamed rice and a variety of side dishes, such as vegetables and sambal.

Preparation Time: 30 minutes

Serves: 6

Ingredients:

- 1/2 cup tamarind juice
- 1 kg pork belly, sliced into 1/2-inch-thick pieces
- 2 tbsp vegetable oil
- 2 tbsp palm sugar
- 1 tbsp ground coriander
- 1/2 cup coconut milk
- 1 tbsp ground cumin
- 6 skewers
- 1 tbsp ground turmeric
- 1 tbsp salt

xxxxxxxxxxxxxxxxxxxxxxxxxxxxxxxxxxxxxxxxxxxxx

Instructions:

a. In a mixing bowl, combine tamarind juice, coconut milk, palm sugar, salt, coriander, cumin, turmeric, and vegetable oil. Mix well.

b. Add sliced pork belly to the marinade and mix well. Cover and refrigerate for at least 2 hours or overnight.

c. Preheat grill to medium-high heat.

d. Thread marinated pork belly onto skewers.

e. Grill pork belly skewers for 8-10 minutes on each side, or until fully cooked.

f. Serve hot with steamed rice and sambal sauce.

17. Spiced Pork Tenderloin with Hazelnut Vinaigrette

Spiced Pork Tenderloin with Hazelnut Vinaigrette is a delicious and elegant dish that combines savory and nutty flavors. The pork is coated in a blend of spices and seared to perfection, while the hazelnut vinaigrette adds a tangy and sweet contrast. It's a perfect dish for a special occasion or a fancy dinner party.

Preparation Time: 45 minutes

Serves: 8

Ingredients:

- 2 tsp ground cumin
- Salt and pepper to taste
- 1/2 tsp salt
- 2 tsp smoked paprika
- 1 tsp garlic powder
- 1/2 cup hazelnuts, chopped
- 1 tbsp dijon mustard
- 1/2 cup olive oil
- 1 tbsp honey
- 1/4 tsp black pepper
- 1 tsp ground coriander
- 2 pork tenderloins (about 2 lbs. or 900 g total)
- 1/4 cup red wine vinegar
- 2 tbsp olive oil

xxxxxxxxxxxxxxxxxxxxxxxxxxxxxxxxxxxxxxxxxxxxxxx

Instructions:

    a. Oven temperature should be set at 375°F (190°C).

    b. Cumin, smoked paprika, coriander, garlic powder, salt, and pepper should be combined in a small bowl.

    c. Pork tenderloins should be covered in the spice mixture.

    d. In a big skillet over medium-high heat, warm 2 tablespoons of olive oil.

    e. Pork tenderloins should be seared for 4-5 minutes per side until browned.

    f. Transfer the pork tenderloins to a baking sheet covered with foil.

    g. Bake for 15 to 20 minutes, or until the internal temperature reaches 145°F (63°C), in the preheated oven.

    h. Before slicing, allow the pork to rest for 5 minutes.

    i. Create the hazelnut vinaigrette in the meanwhile. Hazelnuts that have been chopped, red wine vinegar, dijon mustard, honey, and olive oil should all be combined in a blender. Blend until completely smooth.

    j. Add pepper and salt to taste.

    k. Serve the sliced pork tenderloin with the hazelnut vinaigrette.

18. Grilled Pork Chops with Burst Blueberry Sauce

Grilled Pork Chops with Burst Blueberry Sauce is a delightful combination of sweet and savory flavors. The pork chops are seasoned with herbs and spices, then grilled to perfection. The blueberry sauce, made from fresh blueberries, honey, and balsamic vinegar, adds a burst of tangy sweetness to the dish. It's a perfect summer meal that is both easy to prepare and impressive to serve.

Preparation Time: 30 minutes

Serves: 8

Ingredients:

- 1 teaspoon onion powder
- 1/4 cup honey
- 1 teaspoon garlic powder
- 1 tablespoon olive oil
- 1 teaspoon smoked paprika
- 1/4 cup balsamic vinegar
- 1 teaspoon black pepper
- 8 bone-in pork chops (1 inch thick)
- 1 teaspoon salt
- 1 cup fresh blueberries

xxxxxxxxxxxxxxxxxxxxxxxxxxxxxxxxxxxxxxxxxxxxx

Instructions:

a. Preheat grill to medium-high heat.

b. Season pork chops with salt, black pepper, garlic powder, onion powder, and smoked paprika.

c. Grill pork chops for 5-6 minutes per side or until internal temperature reaches 145°F (63°C).

d. While pork chops are grilling, make the blueberry sauce.

e. In a blender, combine blueberries, honey, balsamic vinegar, and olive oil. Blend until smooth.

f. Pour the mixture into a small saucepan and heat over medium heat until it starts to bubble.

g. Reduce heat to low and simmer for 10 minutes, stirring occasionally.

h. Remove from heat and let cool for a few minutes.

i. Serve grilled pork chops with blueberry sauce on top.

19. Spicy Cumin-Braised Pork

Spicy Cumin-Braised Pork is a flavorful and aromatic dish that features tender, slow-cooked pork infused with a blend of bold spices and herbs, including cumin, coriander, and chili powder. The result is a savory and spicy dish that is perfect for a cozy night in or a casual dinner party.

Preparation Time: 2 hours

Serves: 6

Ingredients:

- 1/4 cup chopped fresh cilantro
- 2 onions, chopped
- 1 tsp. salt
- 1 tbsp. paprika
- 2 cups chicken broth
- 4 cloves garlic, minced
- 2 tbsp. cumin
- 2 tbsp. tomato paste
- 2 lbs. pork shoulder, cut into 2-inch pieces
- 2 tbsp. vegetable oil
- 1/2 tsp. black pepper
- 1 tsp. cayenne pepper

xxxxxxxxxxxxxxxxxxxxxxxxxxxxxxxxxxxxxxxxxxxxxxx

Instructions:

a. Set oven temperature to 325 °F (160 °C).

b. A Dutch oven with medium-high heat is used to warm the oil. Approximately 10 minutes after adding the pork, heat it until it is browned on both sides.

c. Pork should be taken out of Dutch oven and placed aside. In the Dutch oven, add the onions and garlic, and simmer for 5 minutes, or until tender.

d. Then, for 1 minute, while continually stirring, add the cumin, paprika, and cayenne pepper to the Dutch oven.

e. Stir the ingredients in the Dutch oven (chicken broth, tomato paste, salt, and black pepper).

f. Return the meat to the Dutch oven and bring the mixture to a simmer.

g. Cover the Dutch oven and transfer it to the preheated oven. Bake for 1 1/2 to 2 hours, or until the pork is tender.

h. Remove the Dutch oven from the oven and sprinkle with chopped cilantro before serving.

20. Crispy Pork Tacos with Red Chile Salsa

Crispy Pork Tacos with Red Chile Salsa are a delicious and satisfying dish that combines crispy pork with a bold and flavorful salsa. The pork is seasoned with spices and fried to perfection, then served in crispy taco shells with a spicy red chile salsa, giving the dish a zesty kick. It's a perfect meal for any occasion.

Preparation Time: 1 hour 30 minutes

Serves: 12

Ingredients:

- 1 tsp salt
- 2 limes, cut into wedges
- 1 tsp black pepper
- 24 corn tortillas
- 2 cups shredded cheese
- 1 tsp cumin
- 1 tsp onion powder
- 2 kg pork shoulder, cut into small cubes
- 2 cups shredded lettuce
- 2 tbsp olive oil
- 1 tsp garlic powder
- 1 cup chopped cilantro

xxxxxxxxxxxxxxxxxxxxxxxxxxxxxxxxxxxxxxxxxxxx

Instructions:

a. In a large mixing bowl, combine the pork shoulder cubes, olive oil, salt, black pepper, garlic powder, onion powder, and cumin. Mix well to coat the pork evenly.

b. Heat a large skillet over medium-high heat. Add the pork and cook for 10-12 minutes, stirring occasionally, until the pork is crispy and browned on all sides.

c. Meanwhile, prepare the red chile salsa by combining the following ingredients in a blender: 2 cups chopped tomatoes, 1 cup chopped red onion, 1 cup chopped red bell pepper, 1/2 cup chopped fresh cilantro, 2 tbsp lime juice, 1 tsp salt, and 1 tsp black pepper. Blend until smooth.

d. Warm the corn tortillas in a microwave or on a griddle.

e. To assemble the tacos, place a spoonful of crispy pork in the center of each tortilla. Top with shredded lettuce, shredded cheese, and chopped cilantro. Drizzle with red chile salsa and squeeze a lime wedge over each taco.

f. Serve immediately and enjoy!

21. Pork Belly Burnt Ends with Barbecue Sauce

Pork Belly Burnt Ends with Barbecue Sauce is a mouthwatering dish that features juicy, tender pork belly cubes coated with a sweet and tangy barbecue sauce. The pork is slow-cooked to perfection, resulting in a crispy, caramelized exterior and a melt-in-your-mouth texture. It's a perfect dish for any barbecue or casual gathering.

Preparation Time: 3 hours

Serves: 6

Ingredients:

- 2 tbsp garlic powder
- 1 kg pork belly
- 2 tbsp onion powder
- 1/4 cup brown sugar
- 1/4 cup honey
- 1 tbsp garlic powder
- 2 tbsp mustard
- 1 cup barbecue sauce
- 2 tbsp paprika
- 2 tbsp smoked paprika
- 1/2 tsp black pepper
- 1/4 cup brown sugar
- 1 tsp cayenne pepper
- 1/4 cup apple cider vinegar
- 2 tbsp chili powder
- 1/4 cup ketchup
- 1/2 tsp salt
- 1 tbsp onion powder
- 1/4 cup Worcestershire sauce
- 2 tbsp salt

xxxxxxxxxxxxxxxxxxxxxxxxxxxxxxxxxxxxxxxxxxxxx

Instructions:

a. Preheat your smoker to 250°F (120°C).

b. Trim any excess fat from the pork belly and cut it into 1-inch cubes.

c. In a mixing bowl, combine garlic powder, brown sugar, paprika, chili powder, salt, and onion powder. Mix well.

d. Add the pork belly cubes to the bowl and toss until they are coated with the seasoning mixture.

e. Place the pork belly cubes on the smoker and smoke for 2 hours.

f. Remove the pork belly cubes from the smoker and wrap them tightly in aluminum foil.

g. Return the wrapped pork belly cubes to the smoker and smoke for another hour or until the internal temperature reaches 200°F (93°C).

h. While the pork belly cubes are smoking, make the barbecue sauce. In a mixing bowl, combine apple cider vinegar, barbecue sauce, honey, ketchup, Worcestershire sauce, brown sugar, mustard, smoked paprika, black pepper, garlic powder, cayenne pepper, salt, and onion powder. Mix well.

i. Remove the pork belly cubes from the smoker and unwrap them from the aluminum foil.

j. Brush the barbecue sauce generously over the pork belly cubes.

k. Return the pork belly cubes to the smoker and smoke for another 30 minutes or until the barbecue sauce is caramelized.

l. Remove the pork belly burnt ends from the smoker and serve hot.

22. Miso-Crusted Pork Roast with Apples

Miso-Crusted Pork Roast with Apples is a flavorful and hearty dish that combines savory miso with sweet and tangy apples. The pork is coated with a blend of miso, honey, and mustard, then roasted to perfection. Served with tender apples, this dish is a perfect balance of savory and sweet flavors.

Preparation Time: 2 hours

Serves: 6

Ingredients:

- 2 teaspoons grated fresh ginger
- Salt and pepper
- 2 tablespoons soy sauce
- 1/2 cup white miso paste
- 2 garlic cloves, minced
- 2 tablespoons honey
- 1 boneless pork loin roast (about 2 kg)
- 2 tablespoons olive oil
- 1/4 cup mirin
- 2 apples, cored and sliced

xxxxxxxxxxxxxxxxxxxxxxxxxxxxxxxxxxxxxxxxxxxxxx

Instructions:

a. Preheat the oven to 375°F/190°C.

b. In a mixing bowl, whisk together the miso paste, mirin, soy sauce, honey, garlic, and ginger.

c. Season the pork roast with salt and pepper, and then spread the miso mixture all over the surface of the roast.

d. Place the roast in a roasting pan and arrange the sliced apples around it.

e. Drizzle the olive oil over the apples and season them with salt and pepper.

f. Roast the pork for about 1 1/2 hours, or until a meat thermometer inserted into the thickest part of the roast reads 145°F/63°C.

g. Remove the roast from the oven and let it rest for 10 minutes before slicing and serving with the roasted apples.

23. Coffee-Cured Pulled Pork

Coffee-Cured Pulled Pork is a unique and flavorful dish that features tender and juicy pork that has been cured with a coffee rub. The result is a rich and smoky flavor that pairs perfectly with a tangy barbecue sauce. It's a perfect meal for a casual gathering or a barbecue party.

Preparation Time: 10 hours

Serves: 2

Ingredients:

- 2 tbsp coffee grounds
- 1 tsp garlic powder
- 1 tbsp salt
- 1 kg pork shoulder
- 1 tbsp brown sugar
- 1/2 cup water
- 1/2 tsp black pepper
- 1 tsp onion powder
- 1 tbsp paprika

xxxxxxxxxxxxxxxxxxxxxxxxxxxxxxxxxxxxxxxxxxxxx

Instructions:

a. Coffee grounds, paprika, brown sugar, salt, onion powder, garlic powder, and black pepper should all be combined in a mixing bowl.
b. Rub the pork shoulder all over with the mixture.
c. Put the water and pork shoulder in a slow cooker.
d. Cook the pork on low for 8 to 10 hours, or until it is very soft and readily shreds.
e. Using two forks, remove the pork from the slow cooker and shred it.
f. Your favorite sides should be served with the pulled pork.

24. Balsamic Pork Chops

Balsamic Pork Chops are a simple yet elegant dish that features juicy and tender pork chops marinated in a flavorful balsamic vinegar and herb mixture. The marinade adds a tangy and sweet flavor to the pork, making it a delicious and easy meal for any occasion.

Preparation Time: 30 minutes

Serves: 4

Ingredients:

- 1 tsp salt
- 4 pork chops (about 1 inch thick)
- 1/4 cup balsamic vinegar
- 1/2 tsp black pepper
- 1/4 cup olive oil
- 1 tsp dried rosemary
- 2 cloves garlic, minced
- 1 tsp dried thyme

xxxxxxxxxxxxxxxxxxxxxxxxxxxxxxxxxxxxxxxxxxxxxxx

Instructions:

a. Set the heat to medium-high on the grill pan or the outdoor grill.

b. Balsamic vinegar, olive oil, garlic, thyme, rosemary, salt, and black pepper should all be combined in a small bowl.

c. Put the pork chops in a big plastic bag that can be sealed, then drizzle the balsamic mixture over them. Seal the bag, then rub the pork chops with the marinade. Allow to marinate for ten minutes at room temperature.

d. Using a meat thermometer, grill pork chops for 5-7 minutes on each side, or until they achieve an internal temperature of 145°F (63°C).

e. Before serving, give the pork chops five minutes to rest.

25. Balinese Sticky Glazed Pork Ribs

Balinese Sticky Glazed Pork Ribs are a mouthwatering and aromatic dish that features tender and juicy pork ribs coated in a sticky and sweet glaze made from a blend of spices, honey, and soy sauce. The result is a flavorful and satisfying meal that is perfect for a casual dinner party or barbecue.

Preparation Time: 1 hour 30 minutes

Serves: 4

Ingredients:

- 1/2 cup soy sauce
- 2 tbsp ginger, grated
- 1/4 cup water
- 1 tsp sesame oil
- 1/4 cup brown sugar
- 2 tbsp hoisin sauce
- 1/4 cup tomato sauce
- 5 kg pork ribs
- 1/4 cup rice vinegar
- 2 tbsp sambal oelek
- 1/2 tsp black pepper
- 1/4 tsp salt
- 4 cloves garlic, minced
- 1/2 cup honey

xxxxxxxxxxxxxxxxxxxxxxxxxxxxxxxxxxxxxxxxxxxxx

Instructions:

a. Preheat oven to 180°C (350°F).
b. Line a baking tray with aluminum foil.
c. Place the pork ribs on the tray and season with salt and black pepper.
d. Cover the tray with aluminum foil and bake for 1 hour.
e. Meanwhile, in a mixing bowl, whisk together soy sauce, honey, brown sugar, rice vinegar, tomato sauce, hoisin sauce, sambal oelek, ginger, garlic, sesame oil, and water.
f. After 1 hour, remove the aluminum foil from the tray and brush the pork ribs with the glaze.
g. Increase the oven temperature to 220°C (425°F) and bake for another 20 minutes, or until the pork ribs are sticky and glazed.
h. Remove from the oven and let it rest for 5 minutes before serving.

26. Soba Bukkake with Chashu Pork and Sesame Vinaigrette

Soba Bukkake with Chashu Pork and Sesame Vinaigrette is a delicious and refreshing Japanese noodle dish. The soba noodles are served cold with tender chashu pork and a flavorful sesame vinaigrette. It's a perfect dish for a hot summer day or a light and healthy meal option.

Preparation Time: 1 hour

Serves: 4

Ingredients:

For the Chashu Pork:

- 2 cloves garlic, minced
- 1/2 cup mirin
- 1 green onion, chopped
- 1/4 cup sugar
- 1 lb. pork belly
- 1/2 cup soy sauce
- 1/2 cup sake
- 1 inch piece of ginger, sliced

For the Sesame Vinaigrette:

- 2 tbsp honey
- 4 cups dashi broth
- 1/4 cup soy sauce
- For the Soba Noodles:
- 1/4 cup sesame oil
- 1/4 cup rice vinegar
- 1 clove garlic, minced
- 8 oz soba noodles
- 1/4 cup chopped green onions
- 1/4 cup chopped cilantro
- 1 tbsp grated ginger

xxxxxxxxxxxxxxxxxxxxxxxxxxxxxxxxxxxxxxxxxxxx

Instructions:

For the Chashu Pork:

    a. Preheat oven to 350°F (175°C).

    b. In a baking dish, combine soy sauce, sake, mirin, sugar, garlic, ginger, and green onion. Mix well.

    c. Add pork belly to the baking dish, making sure it is fully submerged in the marinade.

    d. Cover the dish with foil and bake for 1 hour.

    e. Remove from oven and let cool. Once cooled, slice the pork belly into thin pieces.

For the Sesame Vinaigrette:

    a. In a medium bowl, whisk together rice vinegar, soy sauce, sesame oil, honey, grated ginger, and minced garlic until well combined.

For the Soba Noodles:

    a. Cook soba noodles according to package instructions.

    b. In a large pot, heat dashi broth over medium heat.

    c. Once the noodles are cooked, drain and divide them among 4 bowls.

    d. Pour the hot dashi broth over the noodles in each bowl.

    e. Top each bowl with sliced chashu pork, chopped green onions, and cilantro.

    f. Drizzle each bowl with sesame vinaigrette.

27. Ginger-Sesame Pork Burgers with Slaw

Ginger-Sesame Pork Burgers with Slaw are a flavorful and juicy alternative to traditional beef burgers. The pork is seasoned with ginger, sesame oil, and soy sauce, giving it a savory and slightly sweet flavor. Served on a bun with a crunchy slaw, this dish is a perfect meal for a casual dinner party or barbecue.

Preparation Time: 30 minutes

Serves: 4

Ingredients:

For the burgers:

- 500g ground pork
- 2 tbsp sesame oil
- 2 tbsp soy sauce
- 1 tsp garlic powder
- 4 burger buns
- 1 tbsp honey
- 1/2 tsp black pepper
- 1 tbsp rice vinegar
- 2 tbsp grated ginger

For the slaw:

- 1 tbsp sesame oil
- 2 cups shredded cabbage
- 1/4 cup chopped cilantro
- 1 tbsp honey
- 1 cup shredded carrots
- Salt and pepper to taste
- 1 tsp grated ginger
- 2 tbsp rice vinegar

xxxxxxxxxxxxxxxxxxxxxxxxxxxxxxxxxxxxxxxxxxxxxxx

Instructions:

   a.   Ground pork, soy sauce, sesame oil, ginger that has been granted, honey, rice vinegar, garlic powder, and black pepper should all be combined in a mixing bowl. Mix thoroughly.

   b.   Make patties by dividing the ingredients into 4 equal pieces.

   c.   Over medium-high heat, preheat a grill pan. The burgers should be cooked through after 5 to 6 minutes on each side.

   d.   Make the slaw while the burgers are cooking. Shredded cabbage, carrots, cilantro, rice vinegar, honey, sesame oil, ginger, salt, and pepper should all be combined in a mixing dish. Mix thoroughly.

   e.   The burger buns should be gently toasted on the grill pan for 1-2 minutes.

   f.   Toast the burger buns on the grill pan for 1-2 minutes, or until lightly browned.

   g.   Assemble the burgers by placing the cooked patties on the bottom buns, then adding a generous amount of slaw on top. Cover with the top buns.

   h.   Serve hot and enjoy!

28. Toulouse-Style Cassoulet

Toulouse-Style Cassoulet is a hearty and comforting French stew that features white beans, sausage, and tender pieces of pork cooked in a rich and flavorful broth. The dish is slow cooked to perfection, resulting in a warm and satisfying meal that is perfect for a cozy night in.

Preparation Time: 4 hours

Serves: 12

Ingredients:

- 1 tsp (5 ml) dried thyme
- 4 cloves garlic, minced
- 1 lb. (450 g) garlic sausage, sliced
- 2 celery stalks, chopped
- 1/2 cup (120 ml) breadcrumbs
- 1 lb. (450 g) dried white beans, soaked overnight
- 1/2 tsp (2.5 ml) ground black pepper
- 1 large onion, chopped
- 2 lbs. (900 g) boneless pork shoulder, cut into 2-inch chunks
- 8 cups (2 L) chicken stock
- 1 lb. (450 g) boneless lamb shoulder, cut into 2-inch chunks
- 2 carrots, chopped
- 2 bay leaves
- Salt to taste
- 1/2 cup (120 ml) red wine
- 1/2 cup (120 ml) tomato paste
- 1 lb. (450 g) pork belly, cut into 2-inch chunks
- 1 tsp (5 ml) smoked paprika
- 2 tbsp (30 ml) olive oil

xxxxxxxxxxxxxxxxxxxxxxxxxxxxxxxxxxxxxxxxxxxxxxxx

Instructions:

a. Set the oven to 350 F (175 C).

b. Beans after soaking should be drained and put in a Dutch oven. 2 inches of water should be added to cover the beans. (5 cm). Cook for 30 minutes at a simmer after bringing to a boil over high heat. Beans should be drained and placed aside.

c. With salt and black pepper, season the lamb and pork. Medium-high heat is used to warm the olive oil in a big skillet. Approximately 5 minutes should be spent on each batch of pork and lamb after they are added. A plate should be used to transfer the meat to.

d. Sausage and pork belly should be added to the skillet and cooked for about 5 minutes, until browned. Place the meat on a platter, then put it away.

e. Cook the vegetables for approximately 5 minutes, until they are tender, including the onion, garlic, carrots, and celery. Add black pepper, smoked paprika, thyme, and bay leaves. Stirring continuously, cook for one minute.

f. While continuously stirring, add tomato paste and simmer for 2 minutes. Cook for 2 minutes while continually stirring in the red wine.

g. When it begins to boil, add the chicken stock. Simmer for ten minutes with the heat reduced to low. Take bay leaves out of the heat and throw them away.

h. Transfer half of the cooked beans to a large baking dish. Add half of the cooked meat and half of the vegetable mixture. Repeat with remaining beans, meat, and vegetables.

i. Sprinkle breadcrumbs over the top of the cassoulet. Bake for 2 hours, or until the top is golden brown and crispy.

j. Serve hot and enjoy!

29. Braised Pork Belly with Pickled Radishes

Braised Pork Belly with Pickled Radishes is a delicious and flavorful dish that features tender and succulent pork belly that has been slow cooked in a savory broth. Served with tangy pickled radishes, this dish is a perfect balance of sweet, salty, and sour flavors. It's a perfect meal for a special occasion or a cozy night in.

Preparation Time: 2 hours

Serves: 6

Ingredients:

- 1 tsp sesame oil
- 2 cups chicken stock
- 1 tbsp salt
- 1 cup brown sugar
- 1/2 cup mirin
- 1/2 cup rice vinegar
- 1 cup soy sauce
- 1 cup rice vinegar
- 2 tbsp ginger, grated
- 6 garlic cloves, minced
- 1 bunch radishes, thinly sliced
- 5 kg pork belly, skin on
- 1/2 cup sake
- 1 tsp black pepper
- 1/2 cup sugar

xxxxxxxxxxxxxxxxxxxxxxxxxxxxxxxxxxxxxxxxxxxxxx

Instructions:

a. Set the oven to 160 °C/320 °F.

b. Chicken stock, soy sauce, brown sugar, rice vinegar, mirin, sake, ginger, garlic, black pepper, and sesame oil should all be combined in a mixing bowl.

c. Put the skin-side up pork belly in a Dutch oven. Over the pork belly, pour the mixture.

d. Place the Dutch oven in the preheated oven with the cover on. 1 1/2 hours of cooking.

e. Once the pork belly is cooked and the skin is crispy, remove the lid and simmer it for another 30 minutes.

f. Make the pickled radishes while the pork belly is cooking. Rice vinegar, sugar, and salt should all be combined in a bowl and whisked until the sugar and salt are completely dissolved.

g. Add thinly sliced radishes and toss to coat. Let it sit for at least 30 minutes.

h. Once the pork belly is done, remove it from the Dutch oven and let it rest for 10 minutes before slicing.

i. Serve the pork belly with the pickled radishes on the side.

30. Pork Bakso Dumplings

Pork Bakso Dumplings are a popular Indonesian dish made from a blend of minced pork, spices, and tapioca flour formed into small dumplings. The dumplings are served in a flavorful broth with noodles and vegetables, making for a hearty and satisfying meal that is perfect for any time of day.

Preparation Time: 1 hour

Serves: 6

Ingredients:

- 1/4 cup chopped cilantro (10 grams)
- 1/2 teaspoon ground white pepper (1.5 grams)
- 1 tablespoon oyster sauce (15 milliliters)
- 1/2 teaspoon salt (2.5 grams)
- 1 pound ground pork (453.6 grams)
- 1 egg, lightly beaten
- 3 cloves garlic, minced
- 1/2 cup chopped scallions (50 grams)
- 1 tablespoon soy sauce (15 milliliters)
- 1 package wonton wrappers (48 pieces)
- 1 cup breadcrumbs (120 grams)

xxxxxxxxxxxxxxxxxxxxxxxxxxxxxxxxxxxxxxxxxxxxxx

Instructions:

a. Combine the ground pork, breadcrumbs, scallions, cilantro, garlic, soy sauce, oyster sauce, white pepper, salt, and the beaten egg in a large mixing bowl. Mix thoroughly.

b. A spoonful of the pork mixture should be placed in the middle of a wonton wrapper. The wrapper is folded in half, and the edges are sealed by pushing them together. Continue using the pork mixture until it is all gone.

c. Bring a big saucepan full of water to a boil. A steamer basket should be placed on the pot.

d. Make sure the dumplings are not touching when you arrange them in the steamer basket. Once the dumplings are cooked through, steam them for 10 to 12 minutes with the lid off the pot.

e. Serve hot with dipping sauces like soy or chili oil.

Conclusion

Congratulations on completing your journey of learning how to cook pork recipes! With your dedication, perseverance, and hard work, you have achieved a significant milestone in your culinary skills.

Your pork recipes cooking book is a testament to your passion for cooking, and it will undoubtedly inspire many others to try their hand at creating delicious pork dishes. Your attention to detail, creativity, and innovative ideas have made this book an invaluable resource for pork lovers everywhere.

The hours of research, experimentation, and taste-testing have paid off, and your pork recipes are now well-crafted and polished. You should be proud of your accomplishment and the impact it will have on the lives of those who use your recipes.

So, congratulations again on this fantastic achievement, and I wish you all the best as you continue to grow and explore new horizons in the world of cooking.

Thank you – Thank you – Thank you

I am grateful to you for purchasing and reading my book. It brings me great joy to write, and my motivation stems from my desire to help others. Writing allows me to achieve this goal, and I am grateful for the opportunity to do so.

May I ask what led you to choose this particular book? With so many books and authors exploring similar topics, it means a lot that you chose mine. Your decision is truly appreciated, and I am confident that you will find the book to be immensely beneficial.

I would love to hear your thoughts on the book. As authors, we grow and improve based on the feedback we receive from our readers. Even a small comment or review would be greatly appreciated. Your feedback could even serve as inspiration for other readers. Thank you once again for your support.

Terra Compasso Bio

Terra Compasso is a cookbook author and food blogger. Born and raised in Italy, Terra's passion for food was kindled at a young age as she watched her grandmother cook traditional Italian meals in their kitchen. Terra worked as a chef in some of the restaurants in Italy. Her love for travel and adventure has influenced her cooking style, as she draws inspiration from the diverse flavors and techniques of different cultures.

Terra's unique approach to cooking has earned her a dedicated following of food enthusiasts who appreciate her emphasis on fresh, locally sourced ingredients and her commitment to sustainability. Her blog offers readers a glimpse into her culinary world, featuring recipes, cooking tips, and stories from her travels.

Whether she's in the kitchen experimenting with new flavors or exploring the markets of a foreign city, Terra's love for food is contagious, and her cookbooks are a reflection of her passion for sharing her culinary adventures with others.

Printed in Great Britain
by Amazon

5758de0b-1669-4442-9f7b-e2571c08b0c5R01